The **Face** of **God**

The Face of God

Woodrow Kroll

President & Bible Teacher
BACK TO THE BIBLE

Copyright ©2004 Elm Hill Books, an imprint of J. Countryman®, a division of Thomas Nelson, Inc.
Nashville, TN 37214

All rights reserved. No part of this book may be reproduced, stored in a retrieval system, or transmitted in any form or by any means—electronic, mechanical, photocopying, recording, or any other—except for brief quotations in printed reviews, without prior written permission of the publisher.

The quoted ideas expressed in this book (but not scripture verses) are not, in all cases, exact quotations, as some have been edited for clarity and brevity. In all cases, the author has attempted to maintain the speaker's original intent. In some cases, quoted material for this book was obtained from secondary sources, primarily print media. While every effort was made to ensure the accuracy of these sources, the accuracy cannot be guaranteed.

For additions, deletions, corrections, or clarifications in future editions of this text, please contact Paul Shepherd, Executive Director for Elm Hill Books. Email pshepherd@elmhillbooks.com.

Scripture quotations are taken from:

The Holy Bible, King James Version (KJV)

The Holy Bible, New King James Version (NKJV) Copyright © 1982 by Thomas Nelson, Inc. Used by permission.

Cover Design by Mark Ross
Page Layout by Bart Dawson

ISBN 1-4041-8504-6

Printed In the United States of America

Table of Contents

Introduction

Usually, we don't identify each other by height, by weight, or by attire; we identify each other by face. Talking with people face to face offers the possibility of intimacy. And, of course, there's nothing quite like seeing the faces of the people we love. This is precisely how God feels: He wants us to seek His face. Why? Because He wants us to know Him in an intimate and personal way.

The faces of the people we meet provide us with important information—information about who they are, how they feel, and how they are likely to behave. And so it is with the face of God. When we sincerely seek to know the face of our Father in heaven, we learn important information about Him and about how He expects us to conduct ourselves.

It is true that God is Spirit and that He doesn't possess a "face" that we human beings might identify by sight. But we must realize that the Bible often speaks to us in language that is anthropomorphic. That is, the Bible uses familiar terms to describe spiritual truths. Describing God's face is one such anthropomorphism.

If we genuinely want to know God, we must spend time with God. In a manner of speaking, we must spend time standing before the face of God. And this book is intended to help.

This text examines the face of God through 31 devotional readings. Each brief chapter contains a Bible verse, an essay, quotations from noted Christian thinkers, and a prayer. The ideas on these pages are powerful reminders that God's face is always turned toward you. Your responsibility—as a believer who has received the gift of salvation from God's only begotten Son—is to make certain that your face and your heart are always turned toward Him.

1

Looking into the Face of God

The LORD bless you and keep you;
The LORD make His face
shine upon you,
And be gracious to you.
Numbers 6:24, 25 NKJV

*T*he Bible clearly teaches the desirability of looking into the face of God. In 1 Chronicles 16, David offers a psalm of thanksgiving and praise. Look at the string of joy in this psalm, beginning with verse 8. "O give thanks to the LORD." The very first stanza opens with thanksgiving before the Lord God. The next bead in this string is: "Call upon his name." After we thank the Lord for who He is, we are instructed to call upon Him so that He may reveal more of Himself. Then, still in verse 8, David talks about witnessing for the Lord: "Make known His deeds among the people" (KJV).

The psalm continues: "Sing unto Him, sing psalms unto Him" (v. 9 KJV). In the previous verse, David had talked about giving thanks to the Lord. Now he instructs us to sing to the Lord. In the remainder of verse 9, David also reminds us to tell of God's wonderful deeds.

The question you might ask is this: "How do I do that?" The answer to that, surprising though it may be, is: you must stop! If you are lost in the desert, the first thing you must do is to stop wandering around! And so it is when you find yourself lost in a spiritual desert: You must stop wandering, and you must be still before the face of God.

You simply cannot be holy and be in a hurry.

Instead, you must spend time alone with God. It may not be easy to find that time, but find it you must. God will refresh you when you take the time to stop, to sit, to be still, and to look into His face.

Get yourself into the presence of the loving Father.
Just place yourself before Him, and
look up into His face; think of His love,
His wonderful, tender, pitying love.

Andrew Murray

Enjoying God's immediate presence, face to face,
is the Christian's highest aspiration.

R. C. Sproul

All praise to our redeeming Lord, who joins us by
His grace and bids us, each to each
restored, together seek His face.

Charles Wesley

To love another person
is to see the face of God.

–

Victor Hugo

A Prayer

*Dear Lord, You are with me always.
Help me feel Your presence in every
situation and every circumstance.
Today, Dear God, let me feel You
and acknowledge Your presence,
Your love, and Your Son.
Amen*

2

Seeking the Face of God

Glory in His holy name:
let the hearts of those rejoice
who seek the LORD.
Seek the LORD and His strength,
seek His face evermore.
1 Chronicles 16:10, 11 NKJV

*A*s we continue to read in 1 Chronicles 16, we encounter these instructions from David: "Glory in His holy name: let the hearts of those rejoice who seek the LORD" (v. 10 NKJV). When we get to know God, when we genuinely come to know who He is, we can relish in the fact that we belong to Him. We glory in Him. In the following verse, David says, "Seek the LORD and His strength, seek His face evermore." Again, we are instructed to seek the Lord. We must seek His strength; we must seek His face; and we must do so continually, without hesitation and without ceasing.

In the church today, I've noticed that we've learned to sing, to shout, to clap, to dance, and to wave our hands, but we really haven't learned to enjoy sitting before the face of the Lord—just communing with the Father, simply seeking Him. And that's a shame.

Whenever we become too busy to "be" with God, we must slow down and we must rearrange our priorities. Why? Because God instructs us to seek His face continually, not simply when we find it easy or convenient to do so.

Today, let's quiet ourselves as we seek the face of God. And then let's continue to do so every day hereafter.

The God we seek is a God who is intrinsically
righteous and who will be so forever.
With His example and His strength,
we can share in that righteousness.

Bill Hybels

Let us humble our hearts before the Lord and
seek his help and approval above all other things.

Jim Cymbala

So I say to you, seek God, and discover Him and
make Him a power in your life. With Him we are
able to rise from the midnight of desperation
to the daybreak of joy.

Martin Luther King, Jr.

God is everything. My focus must be on him,
seeking to know him more completely and
allowing him full possession of my life.

Mary Morrison Suggs

Mark it down. God never turns away
the honest seeker. Go to God with
your questions. You may not find all
the answers, but in finding God,
you know the One who does.

–

Max Lucado

A Prayer
*How comforting it is, Dear Lord, to
know that if I seek You, I will find You.
You are with me, Lord, every step
I take. Today and every day, Father,
I will praise You for revealing
Your Word, Your way, and Your love.
Amen*

3

The Loving Face of God

*And we have known and believed
the love that God has for us.
God is love,
and he who abides in love
abides in God, and God in him.*
1 John 4:16 NKJV

*J*im Elliot was a man whom God used in a mighty way; then God took him home at an early age. Jim understood what it meant to be in love with the Lord God, what it meant to seek the face of the Father. Elliot said, "O the fullness, pleasure, sheer excitement of knowing God on earth. I care not if I never raise my voice again for Him, if only I may love Him, please Him. Perhaps in mercy He shall give me a host of children that I may lead them through the vast star fields of the universe to explore His delicacies, whose finger ends set them all burning. But if not, if only I may see Him, touch His garments, smile into His eyes—ah, then not stars nor children shall matter, only Himself."

These words remind us of the glorious pleasures can be ours when we genuinely seek the presence of our loving God. So today, as a way of participating in the love that can be yours in Christ, look into the loving face of God. Your Heavenly Father is waiting patiently for you to "smile into His eyes." Don't make Him wait a single minute longer.

May you and I be more and more drawn in,
taken over, and consumed by this love from God.

Richard Foster

Though we may not act like our Father,
there is no greater truth than this:
We are his. Unalterably. He loves us. Undyingly.
Nothing can separate us from the love of Christ.

Max Lucado

Believing that you are loved will set you free
to be who God created you to be.
So rest in His love and just be yourself.

Lisa Whelchel

The essence of God's being is love—
He never separates Himself from that.

Kay Arthur

Love so amazing, so divine,
demands my soul, my life, my all.

–

Isaac Watts

A Prayer

God, You are love. I love You, Lord,
because of Your great love for me.
And, as I love You more, Lord,
I am then able to love my family and
friends more. Let me be Your loving
servant, Heavenly Father, today
and throughout eternity.
Amen

4

Finding Joy in the Face of God

*These things I have spoken to you,
that My joy may remain in you,
and that your joy may be full.*
John 15:11 NKJV

*I*f all of God's attributes are infinite (infinite love, infinite grace, infinite mercy), then God's joy must be infinite as well. And better yet, it's contagious. Jesus said that He wanted His joy to be in us! Where do we find this joy? We find it in God's face. There is no joy on earth like the joy of spending an intimate hour alone with the Lord.

A little boy was in the worship service one Sunday. He was turned around in his seat facing the people behind him. He wasn't gurgling, spitting, talking, humming, or tearing pages out of the hymnal. He was simply smiling at the people behind him. When the mother discovered this, she was concerned about matters of etiquette, as mothers tend to be. She jerked him around and said, "Stop grinning! This is church."

I hope that we can start grinning again because it is church—a place where we should experience the joyful presence of the face of God.

As I contemplate all the sacrifices required in
order to live a life that is totally focused on
Jesus Christ and His eternal kingdom,
the joy seeps out of my heart onto my face
in a smile of deep satisfaction.

Anne Graham Lotz

When Jesus Christ is the source of our joy,
no words can describe it.

Billy Graham

In the absence of all other joys,
the joy of the Lord can fill the soul to the brim.

C. H. Spurgeon

Joy is the serious business of heaven.

C. S. Lewis

God gives to us a heavenly gift
called joy, radically different in quality
from any natural joy.

–

Elisabeth Elliot

A Prayer

*Heavenly Father, today let the joy of
the Lord be my strength. I rejoice in
the day You have made. I have joy as
I spend time before your face. The life
You have given me in Christ is full and
wonderful. I rejoice in everything,
I can do no other.
Amen*

5

Finding Strength in the Face of God

He gives power to the weak, and to those who have no might He increases strength. Even the youths shall faint and be weary, and the young men shall utterly fall, but those who wait on the LORD shall renew their strength; they shall mount up with wings like eagles, they shall run and not be weary, they shall walk and not faint.

Isaiah 40:29–31 NKJV

*W*hen we sincerely seek the face of God, we gain strength. And when we do, we stand in a long line of people who have sought the same sense of strength . . . and found it.

Noah sought the face of the Lord God, and he found strength to be buoyed up during the days of the great flood. Moses sought the face of the Lord, and he found strength to lead the Israelites out of Egypt. David sought the face of the Lord God, and he discovered the strength to win the battle over the great giant, Goliath. Daniel sought the strength of the Lord God, and he spent a whole night in the lions' den with no harm.

After denying His Lord, Peter sought God's face and God brought him back from serious defeat to great victory. Peter became the principal preacher of Christianity to the Jews in the early New Testament church. Paul sought the face of the Lord God; he pioneered the penetration of the Gospel into the Gentile world.

Martin Luther sought the face of the Lord God. In His strength, this obscure monk in a tiny village in northern Germany stood up against a very powerful church and the Protestant Reformation began.

In 1939, a young preacher named Theodore Epp understood what it meant to find God's strength. He came to Lincoln, Nebraska and began to broadcast on a tiny radio station with only 250 watts of power, the equivalent of three household light bulbs. His broadcast was called Back to the Bible. Back to the Bible is now broadcasting in 23 languages around the world. Its broadcast covers about 85% of the earth's surface every day. If everybody who could tune into the broadcast did tune in, 3.5 billion people every day could hear the Gospel through Back to the Bible—all from a man who found strength in the face of the Lord God.

Strength comes from the time we spend alone before the face of God. Take time to know God face to face; come to know Him intimately. And gain the strength that He alone can offer.

God walks with us. He scoops us up in His arms or simply sits with us in silent strength until we cannot avoid the awesome recognition that yes, even now, He is here.

Gloria Gaither

If all things are possible with God,
then all things are possible to him
who believes in Him.

—

Corrie ten Boom

A Prayer

*Dear Heavenly Father, You are
my strength. When I am troubled,
You comfort me. When I am
discouraged, You lift me up.
When I am fearful, You give me
courage. Let me turn to You when I am
weak. Whatever my circumstances,
Lord, let me look to You for my strength
and my salvation.
Amen*

6

The Rewarding Face of God

But without faith it is impossible to please Him, for he who comes to God must believe that He is, and that He is a rewarder of those who diligently seek Him.
Hebrews 11:6 NKJV

*G*od says there is enjoyment and reward when we seek Him. If we don't make the effort to seek His face, we miss out on the things He has in store for us. So let's think about the rewards and the benefits that are ours when we seek the face of God. But before we do, a word of warning: This is not a "What's in it for me" study. It sounds like it could be an exercise in selfishness, but that's not what we intend. When we seek God's face, it's not His blessings or benefits that we're after. It's God Himself that we should want. The rest comes as a benefit of seeking Him.

Psalm 27 is another one of David's delightful psalms. It begins: "The LORD is my light and my salvation; whom shall I fear? The LORD is the strength of my life; of whom shall I be afraid? (v.1 NKJV)

This is tremendous. And how do we come to know God? We come to know Him through faith in the Lord Jesus Christ. Jesus is our salvation and our strength.

In a world that wavers, in a world that lacks confidence, in a world filled with temptations, God is steadfast. Let us seek His face and receive the rewards that He has promised.

We should live in light of being called out of
this world at any time into the presence of God,
where we will receive our eternal reward.

John MacArthur

Faith is to believe what you do not see;
the reward of this faith is to see what you believe.

St. Augustine

God's creative method is movement,
change, continuing search, ongoing inquiry.
Those who seek are rewarded.

John M. Templeton

The manifold rewards of a serious, consistent
prayer life demonstrate clearly that time
with our Lord should be our first priority.

Shirley Dobson

Freedom is not an absence of
responsibility; but rather a reward we
receive when we've performed our
responsibility with excellence

—

Charles Swindoll

A Prayer
Dear Lord, thank You for the abundant
life that is mine through Christ Jesus.
Guide me according to Your will, and
help me to be a worthy servant through
all that I say and do. Give me courage,
Lord, to claim the rewards You have
promised, and when I do,
let all the glory be Yours.
Amen

7

The Revealing Face of God

For the LORD gives wisdom;
From His mouth come knowledge
and understanding.
Proverbs 2:6 NKJV

A. W. Tozer said, "You will learn more in a quiet hour before the Lord God than in years of seminary training." Now, let me make it clear: I'm all for education. I spent 22 years of my life in education. Education is important, but God's wisdom is far more important. A. W. Tozer was correct: there is simply no substitute for the wisdom we gain when we seek the face of God.

If you sincerely seek to understand God's truth, sit down quietly with your Bible and ask the Spirit of God to reveal to you His truth from the Word. Psalm 119:105 teaches us that "Your word is a lamp to my feet and a light to my path" (NKJV). So today, seek the wisdom that can be yours when you genuinely, humbly, and prayerfully seek the face of God. Spend time in the Bible and let God reveal to you the rich treasures found in His Word. After all, who, in the entire universe, could possibly be a better teacher?

God has spoken by His prophets, spoken
His unchanging Word, each from age to age
proclaiming God, the one, the righteous Lord.

George W. Briggs

God has given us all sorts of counsel and
direction in his written Word; thank God,
we have it written down in black and white.

John Eldredge

God's Word is not merely letters on paper . . .
it's alive. Believe and draw near, for it
longs to dance in your heart and
whisper to you in the night.

Lisa Bevere

The Bible is God's Word, given to us by God
Himself so we can know Him and
His will for our lives.

Billy Graham

God's Word is a light not only
to our path but to our thinking.
Place it in your heart today,
and you will never walk in darkness.

—

Joni Eareckson Tada

A Prayer

*Dear Lord, the Bible is Your gift to me;
let me use it. When I stray from
Your Holy Word, Lord, I suffer. But,
when I place Your Word at the very
center of my life, I am blessed. Make
me a faithful student of Your Word.*
Reveal to me the truths
that are found in it.
Amen

8

Finding Hope in the Face of God

*Let us hold fast the confession
of our hope without wavering,
for He who promised is faithful.*
Hebrews 10:23 NKJV

*L*ook around you. Read the newspaper. Watch the evening news. When you think about the things that are going on in Washington or elsewhere in the world, it's possible to lose hope. But God provides an antidote to despair. One of the benefits of spending time before the face of God is the gift of divine hope.

Have you ever felt your hope in the future slipping away? If so, here's what you should do: study God's Word, seek God's will, and spend prayerful hours before God's face. When you do, you'll discover the hope that is the possession of those who place their trust in Him.

This world can be a place of trials and tribulations, but as believers in Christ we are secure. We need never lose hope because God has promised us peace, joy, and eternal life. So, let us face each day with hope in our hearts and trust in our God. And, let us teach our children to do likewise. After all, God has promised us that we are His throughout eternity, and He keeps His promises. Always.

When you say a situation or a person is hopeless,
you are slamming the door in the face of God.

Charles Allen

Never yield to gloomy anticipation.
Place your hope and confidence in God.
He has no record of failure.

Mrs. Charles E. Cowman

I wish I could make it all new again; I can't.
But God can. "He restores my soul," wrote
the shepherd. God doesn't reform; he restores.
He doesn't camouflage the old; he restores
the new. The Master Builder will pull out
the original plan and restore it. He will restore
the vigor, he will restore the energy.
He will restore the hope.
He will restore the soul.

Max Lucado

Faith is believing God in the present,
and hope is believing God for the future.

John MacArthur

Oh, remember this: There is never a time when we may not hope in God. Whatever our necessities, however great our difficulties, and though to all appearances help is impossible, yet our business is to hope in God, and it will be found that it is not in vain.

—

George Mueller

A Prayer

Today, Dear Lord, I will live in hope. If I become discouraged, I will turn to You. If I grow weary, I will seek strength in You. In every aspect of my life, I will trust You. You are my Father, Lord, and I place my hope and my faith in You.

Amen

9

Finding Courage in the Face of God

The LORD is my light and my salvation;
whom shall I fear?
The LORD is the strength of my life;
of whom shall I be afraid?

Psalm 27:1 NKJV

$\mathcal{D}$ ivine courage comes to those who spend time before the face of the Lord God. Courage comes to those who learn to seek the Lord and trust Him completely.

The rest of this world hasn't yet found a pavilion before the face of God. The rest of this world doesn't know anything about the secret, quiet place of the Most High God. The rest of this world hasn't found the peace and protection that belong to those who believe in Him. We should be different from the rest of the world. As believers who have been transformed and saved by the sacrifice of God's Son, we should live confidently and courageously.

Today, accept the courage that can be yours when you gain intimacy with your Father in heaven. Even if the path seems difficult, even if your heart is fearful, trust your Heavenly Father and follow Him. Trust Him with your day and with your life. Do His work, care for His children, and share His Good News. Look into His face and have courage. He will surely protect you today, tomorrow, and forever.

Daniel looked into the face of God and
would not fear the face of a lion.

C. H. Spurgeon

Courage faces fear and thereby masters it.
Cowardice represses fear and
is thereby mastered by it.

Martin Luther King

Why rely on yourself and fall? Cast yourself upon
His arm. Be not afraid. He will not let you slip.
Cast yourself in confidence.
He will receive you and heal you.

St. Augustine

Courage! In the spiritual life, whoever doesn't go
forward goes backward. It's the same as with
a boat that must always go forward.
If it stands still, the wind will blow it back.

Padre Pio of Pietrelcina

What is courage? It is the ability
to be strong in trust, in conviction,
in obedience. To be courageous is
to step out in faith—to trust and obey,
no matter what.

—

Kay Arthur

A Prayer

*Dear Lord, when I am fearful,
let me lean upon You. You are my God,
my strength, and my shield. With You
by my side, I have nothing to fear.
And with Your Son, Jesus as my Savior,
I have received the priceless gift of
eternal life. Help me to be a grateful
and courageous servant
this day and every day.
Amen*

10

The Unique Face of God

Tell and bring forth your case;
Yes, let them take counsel together.
Who has declared this from ancient time?
Who has told it from that time?
Have not I, the LORD? And there is
no other God besides Me,
a just God and a Savior;
there is none besides Me.

Isaiah 45:21 NKJV

*L*ook into the face of Buddha and what do you see? A warm and gentle individual who is ready to meet your every need? Someone who can help you live life to its fullest? Someone who wants to save your soul? Or do you see a cold and lifeless metal sculpture of a man who died a long time ago—someone who is powerless to even reach out and touch your hand?

Looking at the faces of men sculpted in stone or metal doesn't really offer much hope, does it? Contrast their faces with the face of Jesus and you'll see a world of difference. Jesus is unique.

Consider the words of Matthew 17:1-3:

Now after six days Jesus took Peter, James, and John his brother, led them up on a high mountain by themselves; and He was transfigured before them. His face shone like the sun, and His clothes became as white as the light. And behold, Moses and Elijah appeared to them, talking with Him.

If you compare the shining face of Jesus at the Mount of Transfiguration with the faces of other great religious leaders of our time and of years gone by, you'll discover that Jesus is unique. Jesus came to be the world's Savior. None of the others did that. None of the others could do that, because their faces did not shine with the glory of God. Only Jesus could do that. That's what sets Jesus apart from everyone else.

Jesus is the only Savior this world will ever have. If you want to look into the Father's face, you must look into Jesus' face. It is the shining face of God. There's only one like it in the whole world. When you and I look squarely into the face of Jesus, we are looking into the unique face of God.

Let us see the victorious Jesus: the conqueror of
the tomb, the one who defied death.
And let us be reminded that we, too,
will be granted the same victory!

Max Lucado

The power of the resurrection of Jesus Christ is
a power that could overcome every spiritual
failing, every sin, every weakness,
in one explosive act.

Bill Hybels

As clearly as the horizon divides
the earth from the sky,
so the resurrection divides Jesus
from the rest of humanity.
Jesus Christ is God in human flesh.

-

John MacArthur

A Prayer

*Dear Lord, You sent Your Son as
the Savior of our world. No one else
could have been that Savior. Jesus is
unique. In His strength, I will share
the Good News with all who cross
my path, and I will share His love with
all who need His healing touch.*
Amen

11

The Delivering Face of God

As for God, His way is perfect;
the word of the LORD is proven;
He is a shield to all
who trust in Him.
Psalm 18:30 NKJV

*O*ne of my favorite missionary couples is the Pattons. John Patton and his wife served in what was once called the New Hebrides Islands in the South Pacific. One story says that shortly after they arrived there, these dear saints of God had their lives threatened by local natives. One night, the local chief and his warriors surrounded the Patton's missionary compound. The warriors carried torches, intending to burn down the compound and kill the Pattons.

The Patton's were absolutely terrified. So they held each other in fear, and they began to pray. They prayed all night long, and when the morning came, the warriors were gone.

About a year later, the chief trusted Jesus Christ as his Savior. John Patton said, "Chief, I must ask you a question. Do you remember a year ago when your warriors surrounded our compound?"

The chief said, "Yes, I remember that."

John continued, "Were you actually going to kill us that night?"

When the chief responded affirmatively, John asked, "What kept you from burning down our compound?"

The chief replied, "All those men."

Patton was puzzled: "What men?"

The chief's reply was straightforward: "All those men with swords and shields that stood around your house. Those are the men that kept us from burning down your house that night."

There were no "men with swords and shields" protecting the Pattons that night, at least not the kind of men who are normally seen. The Spirit of God had sent His angels to deliver His servants.

When God turns His face upon us, it means deliverance. Sometimes it is God's intent for us to go through difficult times—sometimes it's God's intent for us to be removed from difficult times. Whichever happens, there is deliverance. And it comes from God.

He goes before us, follows behind us,
and hems us safe inside the realm
of His protection.

Beth Moore

We can take great comfort that
God never sleeps—so we can.

Dianna Booher

The Lord God of heaven and earth,
the Almighty Creator of all things, He who
holds the universe in His hand as though it
were a very little thing, He is your Shepherd,
and He has charged Himself with the care and
keeping of you, as a shepherd is charged with
the care and keeping of his sheep.

—

Hannah Whitall Smith

A Prayer

*Lord...You have promised never to leave
me or forsake me. You are always with me,
protecting me and encouraging me. Whatever
this day may bring, I thank You for Your love
and Your strength. Let me lean upon You,
Father, this day and forever.*

Amen

12

The Restoring Face of God

*The LORD is my shepherd;
I shall not want.
He makes me to lie down
in green pastures;
He leads me beside
the still waters.
He restores my soul.*

Psalm 23:1-3 NKJV

*W*hat does it mean for God to restore our souls? Simply this: The God who loved us, who created us, and who sent His Son to offer us salvation, that God is still with us. And if we have wandered away and haven't looked into God's face for a long time, that same God is waiting to restore us.

There was a little Alpine church in Switzerland whose people came from miles around to hear its organ. The organ played exquisite music. But one day something happened to the organ, and it wouldn't play anymore. The church fathers employed a series of experts, but none could fix the instrument. Finally, a little old man arrived at the door of the church. He said he wanted to try to repair the organ. The man was told, "We've had so many experts here, and they couldn't do it." But the man said, "I think I can."

For two days, the man worked on the organ. Then, on the third day, suddenly the organ began to play. The music was heavenly. Farmers on the hillsides tied up their cows and came down. Shopkeepers in the little village put "Closed" in the window and came to the church to hear the glorious sounds. And everyone asked, "How could this man repair the organ when no one else could?" Their question was answered when they discovered that fifty years earlier, the same little man had built the organ and installed it in their church.

The Creator can restore us like no one else can. So, if you're looking for restoration, the place to go is to the One who created you. If you've wandered from the Lord, God's face is still shining. Look into that shining face. It welcomes you back to intimacy with Him. God can deliver you and restore you. Ask, and you will receive.

The Scripture is abundant and clear:
Christ came not only to pardon us, but also
to heal us. He wants the glory restored.

John Eldredge

Repentance removes old sins and wrong attitudes,
and it opens the way for the Holy Spirit
to restore our spiritual health.

Shirley Dobson

He is the God of wholeness
and restoration.

–

Stormie Omartian

A Prayer

*Dear Lord, sometimes I grow weary;
sometimes I am discouraged;
sometimes I am fearful. Yet when I turn
my heart and my prayers to You,
I am restored. Renew my strength,
Father, and let me draw comfort and
courage from Your promises
and from Your unending love.
Amen*

13

The Hidden Face of God

*Wait on the LORD;
Be of good courage,
and He shall strengthen your heart;
Wait, I say, on the LORD!*
Psalm 27:14 NKJV

*W*here is God when bad things happen? Where is God when a child is diagnosed with leukemia? Or when a teenage neighbor is killed by a drunk driver? Where is God when a flood or an earthquake wipes out people in their homes? When a gifted pastor is broken by sin? When terrorists attack? Where is God when...? It's a question often asked. When calamity strikes, we want to know, *why?*

Our thoughts about the face of God, up to this point, have been quite positive. Yet we must also acknowledge the fact that some aspects of God's face are, from our perspective, not so pleasant to consider. Indeed, God, on occasion, does hide His face from us completely.

In Job we read "When He gives quietness, who then can make trouble? And when He hides His face, who then can see Him, whether it is against a nation or a man alone?" (34:29 NKJV) This passage overwhelms us with the possibility that God can keep us from seeing His face. In fact, God can hide His face from us and, at the same time, pay very close attention to us.

So what does God do when He hides His face? When we examine the entire chapter of Job 34, it appears that one thing God does when He hides His face is this: He examines the sins of the people. In other words, God shuts off contact with us to engage in a kind of divine surveillance. He's watching us so that He can inspect our sins. May we, as believers in a just and loving God, behave accordingly.

God's delays and His ways can be confusing because the process God uses to accomplish His will can go against human logic and common sense.

Anne Graham Lotz

God never hurries. There are no deadlines against which He must work. To know this is to quiet our spirits and relax our nerves.

A. W. Tozer

God is in no hurry. Compared to the works of mankind, He is extremely deliberate. God is not a slave to the human clock.

Charles Swindoll

Waiting means going about
our assigned tasks, confident that
God will provide the meaning
and the conclusions.

–

Eugene Peterson

A Prayer

*Heavenly Father, when You hide
Your face, let me wait quietly for You.
May I live according to Your plan
and according to Your timetable.
Dear Lord, even when I can't see You
in the circumstances around me,
help me to continually trust in You
and in Your master plan.
Amen*

14

The Convicting Face of God

And when He has come,
He will convict the world of sin,
and of righteousness,
and of judgment.
John 16:8 NKJV

*M*odern spy technology is so advanced that an orbiting satellite can zero in on something that's no more than 36 inches square on the earth's surface. If man's surveillance is that good, imagine what divine surveillance is like. God can see through, over, and under everything. When God is not responding to us, it may be that He is hiding His face while He is examining us. Sometimes God hides His face from us while He examines our sin.

In Deuteronomy 31, beginning at verse 16, we learn that sometimes God hides His face from us, not only to examine our sin but also to expose our sin. Sometimes God hides His face from us—and sometimes He withholds His blessings—because we have not dealt with sin in our lives. His intent is to examine our sins and to convict us of them.

Now, you may be thinking, "I certainly didn't need to hear that today. Tell me some good news." Well here it is: When God begins to expose and convict us of sin, it is for our good. Sin hurts us, so the sooner we submit to God's conviction and repent of our sin, the happier we'll be.

Has God been speaking to you about some sin in your life? Then confess it, turn from it and get back on track with Jesus.

Conviction is worthless until it is converted
into conduct.

Thomas Carlyle

Every secret act of character, conviction,
and courage has been observed in living color by
our omniscient God.

Bill Hybels

A new view of God's holiness gives a deeper view
of our sinfulness. The more we realize a God
of glory, the more we feel our unholiness
and cry out in fear. Woe is me!
Conviction must come before cleansing..

Horatius Bonar

A diffuse and vague guilt feeling kills
the personality, whereas the conviction of sin
gives life to the personality. The former depends
on people, on public opinion,
while the latter depends on God.

Paul Tournier

Repentance is an inward conviction
that expresses itself in
an outward action.

–

Max Lucado

A Prayer

*Dear Lord, when there is sin in my life,
let me understand it, let me confront it,
and let me defeat it. Give me strength
when I am weak so that I might keep
Your commandments and honor
Your Son today and every day of my life.
Amen*

15

Confession and the Face of God

*If we say that we have no sin,
we deceive ourselves, and the truth
is not in us. If we confess our sins,
He is faithful and just to forgive us
our sins and to cleanse us
from all unrighteousness.*
1 John 1:8, 9 NKJV

*S*ometimes, God hides His face to bring us to confession. The word "confess" means to agree with. God wants us to come to that point in our life where we are willing to agree with Him that certain actions, thoughts and spoken words are contrary to His will for our lives. As long as we deny that something is a sin, it is impossible to be forgiven. In fact, we don't even seek forgiveness for it because we refuse to admit that it's wrong. And worse yet, we are calling God a liar because He calls it a sin, and we don't.

But confession also presupposes a willingness to turn from that sin. To confess something that you intend to keep on doing is a mockery.

If there's something going on in your life—maybe no one else even knows about it—that causes God to hide His face from you, there is a good answer—a godly answer—to your situation. That answer is found in 1 John 1:9 quoted on the previous page. This passage promises that if you genuinely confess your sins to God, He will forgive you and He will cleanse you from all unrighteousness. Cleansing means that not even the stain of sin will remain in God's sight—it is purged from His mind.

Agree with God that you have sinned and seek His power to cease from this sin. Be as specific as you can. Not simply, "Forgive me all my sins," but name them as God brings them to memory. Then let the blood of Jesus cleanse and restore you to a right relationship with your heavenly Father so that once more you can see His face.

Confession heals, confession justifies, confession grants pardon of sin, all hope consists in confession; in confession there is a chance for mercy.

Isidore of Seville

Prayer is the same as the breathing of air for the lungs. Exhaling makes us get rid of our dirty air. Inhaling gives clean air. To exhale is to confess, to inhale is to be filled with the Holy Spirit.

Corrie ten Boom

True confession of sin is not just
with the lips, for there must also
be a broken heart.

—

Warren Wiersbe

A Prayer

*When I fail to follow Your
commandments, Lord, I must not only
confess my sins, I must also turn from
them. When I fall short, help me to
change. When I stray from You, guide
me back to Your side. Forgive my sins,
Dear Lord, and help me live from
this day forward according to
Your plan for my life.
Amen*

16

The Faith-building Face of God

For in it the righteousness of God
is revealed from faith to faith;
as it is written,
"The just shall live by faith."
Romans 1:17 NKJV

My wife, Linda, has an inherited disease that was recently diagnosed. It's called CADASIL, and though it isn't life-threatening, it is a life-shortening illness. Linda is a help and comfort to me and an inspiration to countless people. When we travel together, folks often shake my hand and say "nice to see ya." Linda, they hug! And I understand why. She's a wonderful person.

So, when we were flying to London in May of 2001 and she awakened dizzy and disoriented, and later we discovered that she had had dozens of mini-strokes, it was easy to ask "Why?" It's a natural response to tough situations. We all do it. David and others do it in the Book of Psalms. We need to understand that God doesn't always answer those sorts of questions. Sometimes He just hides His face from us; and in the process of hiding His face, He's working to grow our faith in Him.

Experiencing God's hidden face is usually a troubling experience. But please understand this: Even when God's face is hidden from you, He loves you still. And because He loves you, God is working for your good. You may not want to see what He examines and eventually exposes—and at times, you may not appreciate the way He causes your faith to grow. But as you look back upon your life, you will discover that the times when God's face was hidden were among the most significant periods in your life.

When we look back on our darkest days, those times when God seemed totally removed, we realize that He never abandoned us—quite the contrary: it was during those difficult times that He did some of His greatest work.

What pleases God is faith, and the weakest faith is better than no faith. Faith does not look at itself. Looking unto Jesus, we find that He meets our needs and proves that we have faith.

Vance Havner

Faith is putting all your eggs in God's basket, then counting your blessings before they hatch.

Ramona C. Carroll

Faith never knows where it is being led,
but it loves the One who is leading.

–

Oswald Chambers

A Prayer

*Dear Lord, Your faithfulness is
complete and perfect. Even when I am
not sure where You are leading me,
I know that Your Son has died for my
sins, and I know that I am protected.
Great is Your faithfulness, Lord.
Help me to be faithful to You today,
tomorrow, and every day of my life.
Amen*

17

The Face of God: Opposing Sinful Places

*Blessed is the man who walks
not in the counsel of the ungodly,
nor stands in the path of sinners,
nor sits in the seat of the scornful;
but his delight is in the law of the LORD,
and in His law he meditates
day and night.*
Psalm 1:1, 2 NKJV

*Y*ou've undoubtedly heard the phrase "a God-forsaken place." Such a place must be desolate, empty and unlivable. It's hard to imagine. Can any place truly be God-forsaken? The answer is yes. There are times when God sets His face against certain wicked places. And those places, because of their wickedness, must bear the brunt of God's wrath.

In Genesis 19 we read the story of Sodom and Gomorrah. These two cities were places where wickedness was rampant. God turned His face in opposition to these dens of iniquity, and He destroyed them. And because we know that God is both just and consistent, we, as citizens of the 21st century, are not exempt. What He has done in the past, He may well do again—and He may well do it to us!

What can we, as individuals, do about the evils that so thoroughly pervade our modern society? We can start by avoiding all the sinful places that God abhors. Next, we can commit our days and our lives to the strict obedience of God's laws. And finally, we must come into a more intimate relationship with God through the person of His only begotten Son, Christ Jesus.

God most surely sets His face against evil places. And in time, He will destroy those places. Our duty is to make sure that we are not there when He does.

Wrath is the dark line in God's face,
and is expressive of His hatred of sin.

Oswald Chambers

I believe in a God of absolute and unbounded
love, therefore I believe in a loving anger of
His which will and must devour and
destroy all that is decayed, monstrous,
abortive in the universe.

Charles Kingsley

It is only the doctrine of the wrath of God,
of His irreconcilable hostility to all evil,
which makes human life tolerable
in such a world as ours.

Stephen Neill

We admire the character of a father who is opposed to disorder, vice, and disobedience in his family, and who expresses his opposition in a proper way. . . . Why shall we not be equally pleased with God, who is opposed to all crime in all parts of the universe, and who determines to express His opposition in the proper way for the sake of preserving order and promoting peace?

—

Albert Barnes

A Prayer

Dear Lord, when I displease You, I do injury to myself, to my family, and to my community. Because sin distances me from You, Lord, I will fear sin and I will avoid sinful places. The fear of sinning against You is a healthy fear, Father, because it can motivate me to accomplish Your will. Let a healthy fear of sin guide my path, today and every day of my life. Amen

18

The Pure Face of God

Blessed are the pure in heart,
For they shall see God.
Matthew 5:8 *NKJV*

*W*henever we observe sin and say, "This is unholy," we may immediately face the accusation that we are judging other people. Some folks are going to say, "You can't judge our lifestyle!" The fact is, we are making a judgment. But we have a standard by which to judge. Some folks will say that we are intolerant. But tolerance is not to be desired when it is in opposition to God's truth.

When we are confronted with evil, we must resist the temptation to "go along with the crowd." We must, instead, turn our hearts and our minds toward the holy face of God, and we must behave accordingly.

God loves sinners. But if we think that because of God's love for sinners that He does not set His face against sinful places, we need to go back to the Bible. Fire and brimstone rained down upon Sodom and Gomorrah because God set His face against these sinful places.

How much sin does it take before God permanently turns away His face? I can't answer that. God is gracious. He is longsuffering. He puts up with a lot. That we know. But there is a line that is crossed when God no longer looks mercifully on the sinner and He turns away His face to judgment. We must keep short accounts with God so that we don't even come close to that line.

Pray for friends and family members who are flirting with God's judgment, whatever their sins. Plead with them to abandon their sinful lifestyles; plead with God to be gracious. And remember: If you or someone you know have turned away from God, into whatever sin, there is hope. God is loving and forgiving. But there comes a time when sin is so blatant, so "in God's face," that, as a Holy Being, He must respond with holy judgment. At some point, persistent sin will exceed God's grace. There is a point of no return. But until that time, plead for mercy, plead for grace. Those trapped in persistent sin, whatever the sin, must come to the place of repentance and submission. That's when God's grace can "kick in" and forgiveness is the result.

Religious activity can never substitute
for a heart that is pure before Him.

Henry Blackaby

Holiness is not an impossibility
for any of us.

–

Elisabeth Elliot

A Prayer

Holy, Holy, Holy...
You are a Righteous and Holy God
who demands that I seek to be
pure and righteous. Forgive me where
I have failed Lord, and renew
a right spirit and holiness within me.
Amen

19

The Face of God: Opposing Sinful People

For the LORD knows the way of the righteous, but the way of the ungodly shall perish.
Psalm 1:6 NKJV

*I*t's easier to picture God as a loving grandfatherly type who has no teeth and no power, but it's wrong. God is holy, and because of His holiness, He sets His face firmly against not only sinful places but also sinful people.

In Leviticus 20:6, we read, "And the person who turns to mediums and familiar spirits, to prostitute himself with them, I will set My face against that person and cut him off from his people" (NKJV). Let us not deceive ourselves: mediums, wizards, and witches are not a thing of the past.

Did you know there are at least 12 million people in the United States who think that their lives are directly impacted by the alignment of planets millions of miles away from them? Twelve million people! They keep no less than 175,000 part-time and 10,000 full-time astrologers working every day. Did you know that there are more psychics than medical doctors in the country of France?

If you think that God condones sin, think again. If you think that God approves of those who engage in wizardry, horoscopes, child abuse, adultery, or any other sin, you are profoundly mistaken. God takes all sin seriously. He doesn't make any distinctions when He says in Psalm 34:16, "The face of the

LORD is against those who do evil" (NKJV). In this passage God doesn't talk about specific evils. It simply says that God's face is set against all those who oppose His will and wishes. That includes all of us and that includes all of our sins.

A person who deliberately and habitually sins is proving that he does not know Christ and therefore cannot be abiding in Him.

Warren Wiersbe

Whatever weakens your reason, impairs the tenderness of your conscience, obscures your sense of God, or removes your relish for spiritual things—that is sin to you.

Susanna Wesley

"Sin" refers to any attitude or action that fails to radiate God's own character.

Stanley Grenz

Surely if we remembered that God sees us when we sin, we would never do what displeases Him.

—

St. Jerome

A Prayer

Holy Father, let my thoughts and my deeds be pleasing to You. I thank You, Lord, for Jesus, the One who took away my sins. Today and every day, I will follow in His footsteps so that my life can be a living testimony to Your love, to Your forgiveness, and to Your Son.
Amen

20

The Abused Face of God

*Then they spat in His face
and beat Him; and
others struck Him
with the palms of their hands.*
Matthew 26:67 NKJV

*T*he great Bible expositor Frederick Farrar wrote a book entitled *The Life of Christ*. In that book, Farrar notes that first century executions were not like modern ones; the authorities did not seek a quick, painless death to preserve a small measure of dignity for the criminal. To the contrary, executioners sought to inflict agonizing torture and complete humiliation. Such was the torture that our Lord Jesus endured for us.

After a prizefighter has been punched a few times in the eye, the eye closes and the face swells. The abuse that Jesus suffered went far beyond that. It's little wonder that by the time Jesus got to the cross, He was barely recognizable as a man (Isaiah 52:14).

This is what they did to the Savior. The face of God was spat upon and it was pummeled with fists. They also struck Him with the palms of their hands. They slapped the very face of God with their open hands. This is the beating that God's face was subject to before they crucified Him. They did everything they could to disfigure, to disgrace, and to defile Him. And He didn't say a word. As a sheep is dumb before its shearers, Jesus spoke not a word to the people who were beating Him.

The next time you try to imagine what the crucifixion was like, take a long, imaginary look at Christ's face. When you look into the face of Jesus, you see what His torturers did to Him simply because He was the loving Lamb of God who came to die for our sins. My prayer for you is that you will never, ever be able to get that image out of your head. Why? Because until you look into the abused face of God, you cannot begin to appreciate what He accomplished for us at Calvary.

We will never comprehend what it cost our Lord in physical agony to offer His forgiveness to everyone—no exceptions.

Anne Graham Lotz

Come and see the victories of the cross. Christ's wounds are thy healings. His agonies, thy repose. His death, thy life. His sufferings, thy salvation.

Matthew Henry

On a hill far away stood an old rugged cross,
the emblem of suffering and shame;
and I love that old cross where the dearest
and best for a world of lost sinners was slain.
Refrain: So I'll cherish the old rugged cross,
till my trophies at last I lay down;
I will cling to the old rugged cross,
and exchange it some day for a crown.

—

George Bennard

A Prayer

*Father, I am humbled when I realize
that Jesus loved me so much, He was willing
to be abused and then to die on a cross
that I might have life. I want the love of Christ
to so permeate my life that I might even be
able to lay down my life for my friends.*
Amen

21

The Determined Face of God

*The counsel of the LORD
stands forever,
the plans of His heart
to all generations.*
Psalm 33:11 NKJV

*T*hink about how old you are. Go ahead; this won't hurt too much. Got it? Okay. Now, add a year to your age. For example, if you're 35, think 36. Thirty-six years ago, a year before you were even born, God knew you.

Now, try this. Add a zero to that number. No wait. Add two zeros. If the number was 36, make it 3,600. Three thousand, six hundred years ago, God knew you. Awesome!

Now go way back in time. Go back before time itself. God still knew you. Can you even comprehend that? I can't. But there's something even more incredible! Before the foundation of the earth was laid, God knew each of us and His redemption's plan was in place (Matthew 25:34; Ephesians 1:3-10; Revelation 13:8, 17:8). Not only did God know us before He created time, He also knew that He would die for us. And He chose to create the universe (and us) anyway. Talk about a determined God!

Before Adam and Eve were on the face of the earth, God had a plan. He was not taken by surprise when Adam and Eve sinned. He already had a plan that included salvation, a plan that included Jesus' death, His burial, and His resurrection. Nothing can stop the eternal plan of God.

When God determined His will, He didn't check the polls first. He didn't contact George Gallop, CNN, Time, or anyone else. When God determined His will, He didn't ask any of us what we thought. So remember this always: God is determined . . . and He will prevail!

It's incredible to realize that what we do each day has meaning in the big picture of God's plan.

Bill Hybels

The only thing that can hinder us is our own failure to work in harmony with the plans of the Creator, and if this lack of harmony can be removed, then God can work.

Hannah Whitall Smith

We will stand amazed to see
the topside of the tapestry and how
God beautifully embroidered each
circumstance into a pattern for our
good and His glory.

–

Joni Eareckson Tada

A Prayer

*Dear Lord, You have a plan for my life.
Let Your purposes be my purposes.
Let Your will be my will. When I am
confused, give me clarity. When I am
frightened, give me courage. Let me be
Your faithful servant, always seeking
Your guidance for my life. And let me be
a shining beacon for Your Son, Christ
Jesus today and every day that I live.
Amen*

22

The Providing Face of God

*And God is able to make all grace
abound toward you, that you,
always having all sufficiency in all things,
may have an abundance for
every good work.*

2 Corinthians 9:8 NKJV

*H*elen Rosavere, a great missionary stateswoman, served the Lord in an orphanage and hospital in Africa, in what was once called Zaire. I heard her give this testimony, probably 20 to 25 years ago:

A baby was born prematurely at the hospital. The mother died during childbirth, and the father was not around. The baby had a two-year-old sister; both were orphans.

Even though Zaire is near the equator, it does get cold there at night. Without an incubator, there was no way to keep the baby warm. So, they put the baby in a box and put some cotton swabs and other things around the baby. Helen Rosavere sent one of the little girls from the orphanage to get the hot water bottle and fill it with water to put it in the box with the baby. But as the girl was filling the hot water bottle, it burst. So they decided to leave the baby in the box and take turns at night sleeping against it to keep away the draft and to keep the infant warm. Still, there was little hope that the baby would live.

The next morning, after the newborn had lived through the night, Helen went to the regular prayer time she had with the girls at the orphanage. She explained the situation, about how the hot water bottle had broken, and that it didn't look good for the little baby. Then they all began to pray.

Nobody prays like children; nobody gets the heart of God like a child. The children prayed for a hot water bottle. One of the little girls said, "Lord, you know we have to have that hot water bottle today." Please remember that these people were living in the middle of Africa. There was no corner drug store, no Wal-Mart, no place to purchase a water bottle. Yet, one child prayed that a hot water bottle, of all things, would come and that it would come that day. Another little girl chimed in and said, "And Lord, would you please send a little dolly for the two-year-old? She's gonna be so lonely."

That afternoon, while Helen was at the hospital, an unexpected box arrived. She and the girls gathered around to open it. They quickly began taking things out of the box: all kinds of bandages and such. Then, to their joy, they discovered a hot water bottle. Who on earth would send a hot water bottle to somebody in Africa? But there it was in the box. When everyone saw the hot water bottle, the little girl who prayed for the dolly started to rummage around inside the box. And sure enough, she found a little doll, too.

The box had been put together by a lady's missionary society and mailed five months earlier. It arrived on a particular day, a day of God's choosing. Even before it was needed, God was providing. Trust Him to provide for you as well.

God provides for those who trust.
George Herbert

But I'm convinced the best way to cope
with change, ironically enough, is to get to know
a God who doesn't change, One who provides
an anchor in the swirling seas of change.

Bill Hybels

When you live a surrendered life,
God is willing and able to provide
for your every need.

Corrie ten Boom

Does God give us a Christ, and yet
will He deny us a crust?
If God does not give us what we crave,
He will give us what we need.

Thomas Watson

As Christians, we must live a day at a time. No person, no matter how wealthy or gifted, can live two days at a time. God provides for us day by day.

—

Warren Wiersbe

A Prayer

Heavenly Father, You have promised never to leave me or forsake me. You are always with me, providing for me and encouraging me. Whatever this day may bring, I thank You for Your love, for Your strength, and for Your provision. I will lean upon You and trust You, Father, this day and forever.

Amen

23

Timing and the Face of God

*The LORD is good to those
who wait for Him,
to the soul who seeks Him.
It is good that one should hope
and wait quietly for the salvation
of the LORD.*
Lamentations 3:25, 26 NKJV

A person's face often reveals character and personality. It can communicate a sense of determination, purpose, direction, or vision. That's what the face of Jesus revealed as He carried out God's divine plan to redeem us from sin. And that plan, like all of God's intentions, always unfolds according to God's perfect timetable—not an instant before, and not an instant after.

In John 7:30 (NKJV), we read that when Jesus was teaching at the temple, certain people tried to seize Him, but they could not do so. Why? Because it was not yet God's perfect time for Jesus to be taken by the authorities: "Therefore they sought to take Him; but no one laid a hand on Him, because His hour had not yet come." In other words, God had a plan and a timetable. The hour had not yet come for Jesus to be taken to the cross. God's timing was perfect then, and it still is today.

God promises us that He has a plan and that He has an inerant understanding of when that plan will unfold. God is never in a hurry, but He is always on time. So trust Him—not only for His provision but also for His timing.

God manages perfectly, day and night, year in and year out, the movements of the stars, the wheeling of the planets, the staggering coordination of events that goes on at the molecular level in order to hold things together. There is no doubt that He can manage the timing of my days and weeks.

Elisabeth Elliot

To wait upon God is the perfection of activity.

Oswald Chambers

Grass that is here today and gone tomorrow does not require much time to mature. A big oak tree that lasts for generations requires much more time to grow and mature. God is concerned about your life through eternity. Allow Him to take all the time He needs to shape you for His purposes. Larger assignments will require longer periods of preparation.

Henry Blackaby

Events of all sorts creep or fly exactly as God pleases.

William Cowper

When God's people believe and pray, the Lord will provide, but we must learn to wait on him with faithful, obedient hearts until the answer comes.

–

Jim Cymbala

A Prayer

Lord...Your timing is seldom my timing, but Your timing is always right for me. You are my Father, and You have a plan for me. When I am impatient, remind me that You are never early or late. You are always on time, Lord, so let me trust in You...always.
Amen

24

The Forward-looking Face of God

Looking unto Jesus, the author and
finisher of our faith, who for the joy
that was set before Him endured the cross,
despising the shame, and has sat down
at the right hand of the throne of God.

Hebrews 12:2 NKJV

*T*here's another fact that amazes me about the face of God; it is always looking toward the future. When Jesus went to Calvary, He was not looking solely at His suffering, but rather Christ was looking beyond the cross to the joy that would follow. Jesus saw a plan that went well beyond His own crucifixion. Before He was crucified, He could already hear the joy bells ringing in heaven. He was that tuned-in to heaven's program. So He endured.

The apostle Paul reflected this same attitude. He told the Christians at Phillipi, "Brethren, I do not count myself to have apprehended; but one thing I do, forgetting those things which are behind and reaching forward to those things which are ahead, I press toward the goal for the prize of the upward call of God in Christ Jesus" (Philippians 3:13, 14 NKJV).

While what's behind us is important, what's in front of us is even more important. If there are issues in your past that need to be dealt with, then do so—but then move on. Put the past behind you and focus on the future. Today, run your race with endurance, and, like Jesus, look beyond Calvary all the way to glory.

God dwells in eternity, but time dwells in God.
He has already lived all our tomorrows
as he has lived all our yesterdays.

A. W. Tozer

The damage done to us on this earth will never
find its way into that safe city. We can relax,
we can rest, and though some of us can hardly
imagine it, we can prepare to feel safe
and secure for all of eternity.

Bill Hybels

God did not spring forth from eternity;
He brought forth eternity.

C. H. Spurgeon

The unfolding of our friendship with the Father
will be a never-ending revelation stretching
on into eternity.

Catherine Marshall

When did God's love for you begin? When He began to be God. When did He begin to be God? Never, for He has always been without beginning and without end, and so He has always loved you from eternity.

—

St. Francis of Sales

A Prayer

Dear Heavenly Father, may I put behind me the things of my past. Let me put them under the blood of Jesus and move on. You have blessed me with a love that is infinite and eternal. Let me love You, Lord, more and more each day. Make me a loving servant, Dear Lord, today and throughout eternity. And, let me show my love for You by sharing Your message and Your love.

Amen

25

The Heavenly Face of God

*Let your light so shine before men,
that they may see your good works
and glorify your Father in heaven.*

Matthew 5:16 NKJV

*J*ohn and Betty Stamm were two of the early martyrs of our generation. They were missionaries to China and were beheaded for the cause of Christ when the Communists took over. As the Communists led John and Betty away with their hands tied behind their back, someone asked them where they were going. John Stamm said, "I don't know where the guards are going, but I'm going to heaven."

Like Jesus, John and Betty Stamm looked beyond the cross and the grave to seeing their Father's face in heaven. Because John knew what the Bible said, and because he believed in the promises of God, he knew that whatever he had to endure in the next few moments was temporary. But he also understood that his heavenly reward was eternal.

Oftentimes, we don't understand God's plan for us and we don't understand His timetable. So we become impatient. We think God isn't doing the things He should; we think He's not doing things at the right time. We question God's wisdom. But whenever we question God, we must remind ourselves of this fact: God has seen to Calvary and beyond. God's face is determined. He does have a plan, the right plan, the best plan. The completion of God's plan brings glory to Himself, and it sweeps us into glory as well.

Like John and Betty Stamm, you must set your sights on the heavenly face of God. Trust Him for the rest of your life and for the eternity that lies beyond.

Even life's happiest experiences last but a moment, yet Heaven's joy is eternal. Some day we will go to our eternal Home, and Christ will be there to welcome us!

Billy Graham

Has this world been so kind to you that you should leave with regret? There are better things ahead than any we leave behind.

C. S. Lewis

As Catherine of Siena said,
"All the way to heaven is heaven."
A joyful end requires a joyful means.
Bless the Lord.

–

Eugene Peterson

A Prayer

I know, Lord, this world is not my home;
I am only here for a short time.
You have given me the priceless gift of
eternal life through Your Son, Jesus.
Keep the promise of heaven in my
heart, and help me to pass through
this world with joy, with perspective,
with thanksgiving, and
with praise on my lips for You.
Amen

26

The Encouraging Face of God

A word fitly spoken is like
apples of gold
in settings of silver.
Proverbs 25:11 NKJV

*G*od's promises have encouraged believers of every generation. And if we are to be servants who are worthy of God's blessings, we, too, must become a source of encouragement to our families, to our friends, and to the world.

The words that we speak have the power to do great good or great harm. If we speak words of encouragement and hope, we can lift others up. And that's exactly what God commands us to do!

Sometimes, when we feel uplifted and secure, it easy to speak kind words. Other times, when we are discouraged or tired, we can scarcely summon the energy to uplift ourselves, much less anyone else. Yet here's what God intends for us to do: He intends that we look upon His encouraging face so that we, in turn, can share His truth, His wisdom, His love, and His encouragement with others. When we do, we share a priceless gift with the world, and we give glory to God's Son, the One who gave His life for us. As believers, we must do no less.

A pat on the back is only a few vertebrae removed
from a kick in the pants,
but is miles ahead in results.

Ella Wheeler Wilcox

Encouragement starts at home,
but it should never end there.

Marie T. Freeman

Words. Do you fully understand their power?
Can any of us really grasp the mighty force behind
the things we say? Do we stop and think before
we speak, considering the potency
of the words we utter?

Joni Eareckson Tada

Encouragement is the oxygen of the soul.

John Maxwell

We urgently need people who encourage
and inspire us to move toward God and
away from the world's enticing pleasures.

—

Jim Cymbala

A Prayer

*Dear Heavenly Father, because
I am Your child, I am blessed. You have
loved me eternally, cared for me faithfully,
and saved me through the gift of Your
Son, Jesus. Just as You have lifted me up,
Lord, let me also lift up others in a spirit of
encouragement and optimism and hope.
Today and every day, let me share
the healing message of Your Son,
to whatever extent I can be so service
to others, Lord, may the glory be Yours.
Amen*

27

The Serene Face of God

*Through the tender mercy of our God,
with which the Dayspring from on high
has visited us; to give light to those
who sit in darkness and the shadow
of death, to guide our feet
into the way of peace.*

Luke 1:78, 79 NKJV

*T*he face of God offers us serenity and assurance. The beautiful words of John 14:27 give us hope: "Peace I leave with you, My peace I give to you; not as the world gives do I give to you. Let not your heart be troubled, neither let it be afraid" (NKJV). Jesus offers us peace, not as the world gives, but as He alone gives. We, as believers, can accept His peace or ignore it.

When we accept the peace of Jesus Christ into our hearts, our lives are transformed. And then, because we possess the gift of peace, we can share that gift with fellow Christians, with family members, with friends, and with the world. If, on the other hand, we choose to ignore the gift of peace—for whatever reason—we have nothing to share.

Today, claim the inner peace and the spiritual serenity that can and should be yours: claim the peace of Jesus Christ.

The better acquainted you become with God,
the less tensions you feel and
the more peace you possess.

Charles Allen

To know God as He really is—in His essential
nature and character—is to arrive at a citadel of
peace that circumstances may storm,
but can never capture.

Catherine Marshall

A great many people are trying to make peace,
but that has already been done. God has not left
it for us to do; all we have to do is to enter into it.

D. L. Moody

There may be no trumpet sound or loud applause
when we make a right decision,
just a calm sense of resolution and peace.

Gloria Gaither

Christ is not only a remedy for your weariness and trouble, but he will give you an abundance of the contrary: joy and delight. They who come to Christ do not only come to a resting-place after they have been wandering in a wilderness, but they come to a banqueting-house where they may rest, and where they may feast. They may cease from their former troubles and toils, and they may enter upon a course of delights and spiritual joys.

—

Jonathan Edwards

A Prayer

Dear Lord, when I turn my thoughts and prayers to You, I feel Your peace. You are the Giver of all things good, Father, and You give me peace when I draw close to You. Help me to trust Your will, to follow Your commands, and to accept Your serenity, today and forever.

Amen

28

The Searching Face of God

*And we have seen and testify
that the Father has sent the Son
as Savior of the world.*
1 John 4:14 NKJV

The face of God is like a shepherd, continually facing His flock, searching for lost sheep, seeking those who need protection, guidance, and salvation.

God loves us and protects us. In times of trouble, He comforts us; in times of sorrow, He dries our tears. Psalm 147 promises, "He heals the brokenhearted and binds up their wounds" (v.3 NKJV). Such is the healing power of God.

Sometimes, we may feel lost or afraid, but we are never really alone; the face of God is always turned toward us.

Do you feel fearful, or weak, or sorrowful? Are you discouraged or bitter? Do you feel "stuck" in a place that is uncomfortable for you? If so, remember that God is as near as your next breath. So trust Him and turn to Him for solace, for security, and for salvation.

Jesus came down from heaven, revealing exactly
what God is like, offering eternal life and
a personal relationship with God, on the condition
of our rebirth—a rebirth made possible through
His own death on the cross.

Anne Graham Lotz

When I read that Christ Jesus came into the world
to save sinners, it was as if day suddenly broke
on a dark night.

Thomas Bilney

Listen to the Savior. He will show you the face
of God, the good Father.

St. Clement of Alexandria

Do we so appreciate the marvelous salvation of
Jesus Christ that we are our utmost
for His highest?

Oswald Chambers

Anyone can devise a plan by which
good people go to heaven.
Only God can devise a plan whereby
sinners, which are His enemies,
can go to heaven.

–

Lewis Sperry Chafer

A Prayer
Lord, You have sought me out.
You care for me; You comfort me;
You watch over me; and You have
saved me. I will praise you, Father,
for Your glorious works,
for Your protection, for Your love,
and for Your Son.
Amen

29

The Merciful Face of God

For He says to Moses,
*"I will have mercy on whomever
I will have mercy, and I will have
compassion on whomever
I will have compassion."*
Romans 9:15 NKJV

The face of God, when it is turned toward His children, is a merciful face. God's ability to forgive is as infinite as His love. The familiar words of Romans 3:23 reminds us of an important truth: "All have sinned, and come short of the glory of God" (KJV). All of us, even the most righteous among us, are sinners. But despite our imperfections, our Father in heaven offers us salvation from the very moment that we first accept His Son as our personal savior.

God sent Jesus to die a horrific death so that we might have eternal life. God's mercy was demonstrated by the total sacrifice of His Son.

As Christians, we have been blessed by a merciful, loving God. May we accept His mercy. And may we, in turn, show love and mercy to our friends, to our families, and to all whom our Heavenly Father chooses to place along our paths.

Mercy is an attribute of God, an infinite and inexhaustible energy within the divine nature which disposes God to be actively compassionate.

A. W. Tozer

Looking back over my life, all I can see is mercy and grace written in large letters everywhere. May God help me have the same kind of heart toward those who wound or offend me.

Jim Cymbala

God giveth his wrath by weight, but his mercy without measure.

Sir Thomas Fuller

Mercy also, is a good thing, for it makes men perfect, in that it imitates the perfect Father. Nothing graces the Christian soul as much as mercy.

St. Ambrose

The Creator has given to us the awesome
responsibility of representing him to
our children. Our heavenly Father is a God
of unlimited love, and our children must
become acquainted with his mercy
and tenderness through
our own love toward them.

-

James Dobson

A Prayer

*Dear Lord, You have given me so much
more than I deserve. You have blessed me
with Your love and Your mercy.
Help me be merciful toward others, Father,
just as You have been merciful toward me,
and let me share Your love with
a world that desperately needs
Your mercy and Your Son.
Amen*

30

The Inviting Face of God

*As the Lord has called each one,
so let him walk.*
1 Corinthians 7:17 NKJV

*W*hen we genuinely turn our hearts toward the face of God, we feel the sense that He is inviting us to walk with Him. And that's precisely the path that we must follow.

Oswald Chambers, the author of the Christian classic devotional text *My Utmost For His Highest*, advised, "Never support an experience which does not have God as its source, and faith in God as its result." These words serve as a powerful reminder that, as Christians, we are called to walk with God and to obey His commandments. But, we live in a world that presents us with countless temptations to stray far from God's path.

When we behave ourselves as obedient servants, we honor the Father and the Son. When we live righteously and according to God's commandments, He blesses us in ways that we cannot fully understand. So, as this day unfolds, take every step of your journey with God as your traveling companion. Study His Holy Word. Follow His commandments. Support only those activities that further God's kingdom and your spiritual growth. Be an example of righteous living to your friends, to your neighbors, and to your children. Then, reap the blessings that God has promised to all those who accept His invitation of life abundant and life eternal.

When you become consumed by God's call on your life, everything will take on new meaning and significance. You will begin to see every facet of your life, including your pain, as a means through which God can work to bring others to Himself.

Charles Stanley

If God has called you, do not spend time looking over your shoulder to see who is following you.

Corrie ten Boom

The place where God calls you is the place where your deep gladness and the world's deep hunger meet.

Frederick Buechner

The call of God is a call to be human, to embrace our humanity in all of its ambiguity. The call of God is a summons to embark upon a journey of faith whose destiny is not always apparent.

Randall Palmer

When God calls a man, He does not repent of it. God does not, as many friends do, love one day and hate another; or as princes, who make their subjects favorites and afterwards throw them into prison. This is the blessedness of a saint: his condition admits of no alteration. God's call is founded on His decree, and His decree is immutable. Acts of grace cannot be reversed. God blots out his people's sins, but not their names.

—

Thomas Watson

A Prayer

Dear Lord, let me choose Your plans.
You created me, and You have called me to
do Your work here on earth. Today, I choose
to seek Your will and to live it, knowing that
when I trust in You, I am eternally blessed.
Amen

31

Worship and the Face of God

*But the hour is coming, and now is,
when the true worshipers will worship
the Father in spirit and truth;
for the Father is seeking such
to worship Him. God is Spirit,
and those who worship Him must
worship in spirit and truth.*
John 4:23, 24 NKJV

I'm going to make a statement that may surprise you. Here it is: *Everybody here on earth is engaged in the practice of worship.* Now I know what you must be thinking: What about all those sinners who continue to live in sin? How on earth could they be worshipping? Well, I maintain that even the most depraved sinners are engaged in worship. The question is not *if* they worship. The question is *what* they worship.

Some people choose to worship God and His Son Jesus. These people (and I sincerely hope you are among their number) reap the joy, the abundance, and the eternal life that God intends for His children. Other people distance themselves from God by worshiping such things as earthly possessions or personal gratification...and when they do, they suffer.

When we place our desires for material possessions above our love for God—or when we yield to temptations of the flesh—we find ourselves engaged in a struggle that is similar to the one Jesus faced when He was tempted by Satan. In the wilderness, Satan offered Jesus earthly power and unimaginable riches if He would only worship him, but Jesus turned Satan away. Jesus chose to worship God. We must do likewise by putting God first and by worshiping only Him.

Every day provides opportunities to put God where He belongs: at the center of our lives. Let us worship Him—and only Him—today and always.

It's our privilege to not only raise our hands in worship but also to combine the visible with the invisible in a rising stream of praise and adoration sent directly to our Father.

Shirley Dobson

O worship the King, all glorious above,
And gratefully sing His wonderful love.

Robert Grant

God-pleasing worship is deeply emotional and deeply doctrinal. We use both our hearts and our heads.

Rick Warren

Worship is a voluntary act of gratitude
offered by the saved to the Savior,
by the healed to the Healer, and
by the delivered to the Deliverer.

–

Max Lucado

A Prayer

*When I worship You, Lord, You direct
my path and You cleanse my heart.
Let today and every day be a time of
worship and praise. Let me worship
You in everything that I think and do.
Thank You, Lord for the priceless gift of
Your Son, Jesus. Let me be worthy of
that gift, and let me give You
the praise and the glory forever.
Amen*

Thoughts & Reflections

_____

_____

_____

_____

_____

_____

_____

_____

_____

_____

_____

_____

_____

_____

_____

_____

_____

_____

Thoughts & Reflections

_____

_____

_____

_____

_____

_____

_____

_____

_____

_____

_____

_____

_____

_____

_____

_____

_____

Thoughts & Reflections

Thoughts & Reflections

_____

_____

_____

_____

_____

_____

_____

_____

_____

_____

_____

_____

_____

_____

_____

_____